STEM CAREERS

FOOD SCIENTIST

by Karen Latchana Kenney

po**go**

Ideas for Parents and Teachers

Pogo Books let children practice reading informational text while introducing them to nonfiction features such as headings, labels, sidebars, maps, and diagrams, as well as a table of contents, glossary, and index.

Carefully leveled text with a strong photo match offers early fluent readers the support they need to succeed.

Before Reading

• "Walk" through the book and point out the various nonfiction features. Ask the student what purpose each feature serves.

• Look at the glossary together. Read and discuss the words.

Read the Book

• Have the child read the book independently.

• Invite him or her to list questions that arise from reading.

After Reading

• Discuss the child's questions. Talk about how he or she might find answers to those questions.

• Prompt the child to think more. Ask: Do you know anyone who works as a food scientist? What projects has he or she been involved in? Do you have any interest in this kind of work?

Pogo Books are published by Jump!
5357 Penn Avenue South
Minneapolis, MN 55419
www.jumplibrary.com

Library of Congress Cataloging-in-Publication Data

Names: Kenney, Karen Latchana, author.
Title: Food scientist / by Karen Latchana Kenney.
Description: Minneapolis, MN: Jump!, Inc., [2019]
Series: STEM careers | Audience: Ages 7-10.
Includes bibliographical references and index.
Identifiers: LCCN 2018018910 (print)
LCCN 2018019232 (ebook)
ISBN 9781641281850 (ebook)
ISBN 9781641281843 (hardcover: alk. paper)
Subjects: LCSH: Food—Research—Vocational guidance—Juvenile literature. | Food industry and trade—Vocational guidance—Juvenile literature. | Food engineers—Juvenile literature. Classification: LCC TX355 (ebook) | LCC TX355 .K38 2018 (print) | DDC 664.0023—dc23
LC record available at https://lccn.loc.gov/2018018910

Editors: Jenna Trnka and Susanne Bushman
Designer: Michelle Sonnek

Photo Credits: DenisNata/Shutterstock, cover; yacobchuk/iStock, 1; JBryson/iStock, 3, 18; ixpert/Shutterstock, 4 (Earth); Nerthuz/Shutterstock, 4 (space station); NASA, 5; valentinrussanov/iStock, 6-7; Budimir Jevtic/Shutterstock, 8; Skynavin/Shutterstock, 9; Cultura Limited/Superstock, 10-11; BW Folsom/Shutterstock, 12-13 (dinner); Phonlamai Photo/Shutterstock, 12-13 (belt); Pradana/Shutterstock, 14-15; wavebreakmedia/Shutterstock, 16-17; Dragon Images/Shutterstock, 19; InStock/Image Source/Superstock, 20-21; Dimitar Sotirov/Shutterstock, 23.

Printed in the United States of America at Corporate Graphics in North Mankato, Minnesota.

TABLE OF CONTENTS

CHAPTER 1

STUDYING FOOD

It's dinnertime on the International Space Station. What do astronauts eat? Their choices are in packets. They don't even need to be refrigerated! Why?

International Space Station

Food scientists made this food for outer space. Some is **freeze-dried**. Some is powdered. And some is heated and then sealed. These processes **preserve** food for months.

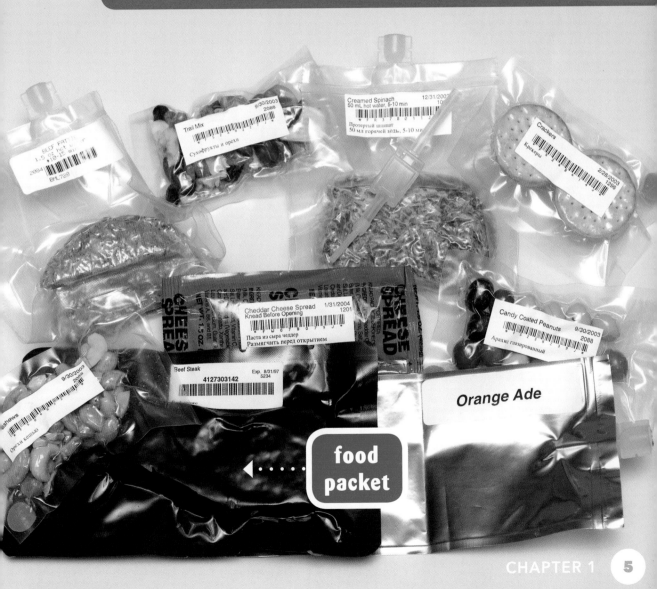

food packet

microscope

Food scientists make sure food is safe to eat. How? They use **microscopes** to study what is in foods. They find out which **microbes** spoil food. These tiny living things make people sick. They include **bacteria**, yeast, and mold.

Their work keeps food items from spoiling. It also helps us know when food is no longer safe to eat. They label food with **expiration dates**.

DID YOU KNOW?

Louis Pasteur was a scientist in the 1800s. He discovered how to kill bacteria in drinks. This process is called **pasteurization**. We use it to keep milk, juice, and other foods fresh and safe to eat.

CHAPTER 2

WHAT DO THEY DO?

Food scientists protect our **food supply**. How? They examine the soil foods grow in and find ways to improve it.

They visit farms and **greenhouses**. They see how foods grow.

greenhouse

We eat many foods. Fruits. Meats. Frozen vegetables. How do food scientists know how to keep all foods safe to eat?

They test food packaging. Does it let microbes in? Does the food stay fresh inside? For how long? They work with engineers. Together, they design better packages.

packaging

They see what happens to foods when they are processed and stored. How? Visiting factories. Checking how vegetables change when they are frozen.

They also help look at the content of food. They tell us what **nutrients** are in foods. They can make food healthier. How? They might add nutrients to foods.

TAKE A LOOK!

The Food and Drug Administration (FDA) makes nutrition labels. These show what is in food. They are changing. How? More information is on them. They are easier to read. See some of the changes!

OLD LABEL

Nutrition Facts

Serving Size 2/3 cup (55g)
Servings Per Container About 8

Amount Per Serving

Calories 230	Calories from Fat 72

	% Daily Value*
Total Fat 8g	**12%**
Saturated Fat 1g	**5%**
Trans Fat 0g	
Cholesterol 0mg	**0%**
Sodium 160mg	**7%**
Total Carbohydrate 37g	**12%**
Dietary Fiber 4g	**16%**
Sugars 12g	
Protein 3g	

Vitamin A	10%
Vitamin C8	%
Calcium	20%
Iron	45%

* Percent Daily Values are based on a 2,000 calorie diet. Your daily value may be higher or lower depending on your calorie needs.

	Calories: 2,000	2,500
Total Fat	Less than 65g 8	0g
Sat Fat L	ess than 20g 2	5g
Cholesterol	Less than 300mg	300mg
Sodium L	ess than 2,400mg 2	,400mg
Total Carbohydrate	300g	375g
Dietary Fiber	25g	30g

NEW LABEL

Nutrition Facts

8 servings per container
Serving size   2/3 cup (55g)

Amount per serving

Calories ❶230

	% Daily Value*
Total Fat 8g	❷**10%**
Saturated Fat 1g	**5%**
Trans Fat 0g	
Cholesterol 0mg	**0%**
Sodium 160mg	**7%**
Total Carbohydrate 37g	**13%**
Dietary Fiber 4g	**14%**
Total Sugars 12g	
❸ Includes 10g Added Sugars	**20%**
Protein 3g	

Vitamin D 2mcg ❹	10%
Calcium 260mg	20%
Iron 8mg	45%
Potassium 235mg	6%

* The % Daily Value (DV) tells you how much a nutrient in a serving of food contributes to a daily diet. 2,000 calories a day is used for general nutrition advice.

❶ bigger **calorie** labels
❷ updated daily values
❸ new added sugars
❹ includes nutrient amounts

How food is grown and made is important to food scientists, too. They do inspections. Of what? **Crops** and **livestock**.

They work with other scientists. Engineers. Even **flavor experts**. They create new food products together, like alternatives to meat and eggs.

Some work at universities. They do research. Others work for the government. Some work for companies that make food, like farms and factories.

DID YOU KNOW?

It is estimated that more than 9 billion people will live on Earth by 2050. Why do food scientists care? They are finding ways to produce more food. This will help feed the growing **population**.

CHAPTER 3

BECOMING A FOOD SCIENTIST

Do you want to make food safer to eat? Do you want to protect our food supply? You could become a food scientist!

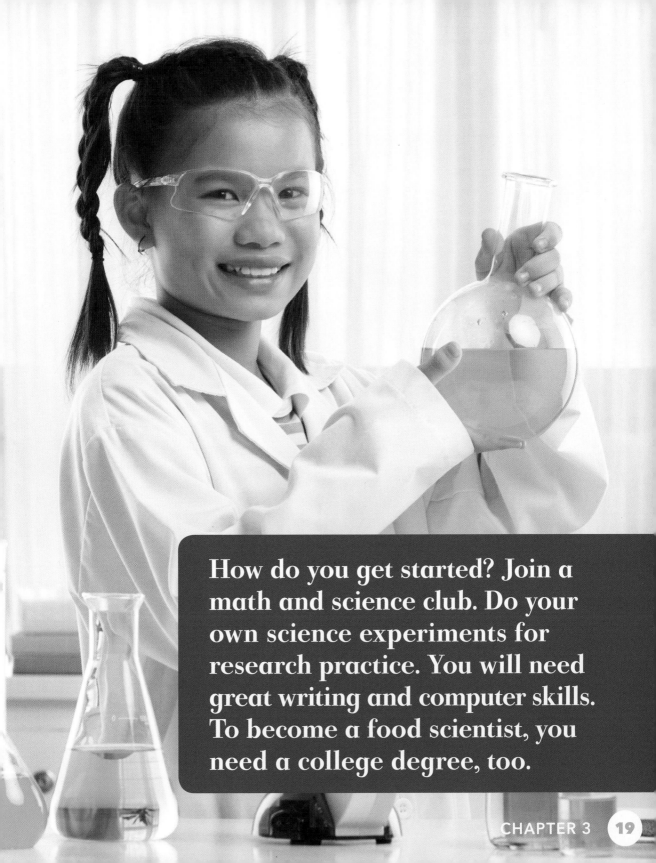

How do you get started? Join a math and science club. Do your own science experiments for research practice. You will need great writing and computer skills. To become a food scientist, you need a college degree, too.

As a food scientist, you can shape the future. How? You can help people stay healthy. And your work will keep the food supply steady. You can help feed our growing world!

DID YOU KNOW?

To work as a food scientist, you need STEM skills. What does STEM stand for? Science. Technology. Engineering. Math. STEM careers are in demand. They pay well, too.

ACTIVITIES & TOOLS

SEE HOW APPLES SPOIL

Food spoils faster and slower under certain conditions. Try this experiment to see what makes apple slices spoil faster.

What You Need:

- 4 glasses
- apple
- knife
- water
- vinegar
- vegetable oil
- labels
- pen

❶ Ask an adult to help you cut the apple into four pieces.

❷ Put an apple piece in each glass. Make four labels: water, oil, vinegar, and air.

❸ Pour water into one glass. Pour vinegar into another. Add oil to the third glass. Make sure the liquids cover the apple slices. The fourth apple slice is covered in nothing but air. Then add labels to the glasses.

❹ Leave the glasses out and check on them each day. Watch what happens to the apple slices. Write down what you see each day.

❺ After one week, ask an adult to help you take the slices out of the liquids. Which slice spoiled the most? Was it in the air, water, vinegar, or oil?

GLOSSARY

bacteria: Tiny living things that may cause diseases.

calorie: A measurement of the amount of energy in a food.

crops: Plants grown for food or feed for animals.

expiration dates: Dates printed on products to tell consumers when the product may spoil or no longer be safe to consume.

flavor experts: Scientists who use chemistry to create or add flavors to food.

food supply: A stock of food that is available to use.

freeze-dried: A process of removing the water from food by freezing it.

greenhouses: Enclosed structures for plants that have controlled lighting and heat so that the plants inside can grow even when it is cold.

livestock: Animals raised for food.

microbes: Germs or other small living things that you can see under a microscope.

microscopes: Scientific tools that magnify very small things so that you can see them.

nutrients: Things people need to have in their food to stay healthy, such as vitamins and protein.

pasteurization: The process of heating liquids, such as milk, to a temperature that kills harmful bacteria.

population: The total number of people that live in a certain place.

preserve: To treat food in different ways so that it does not spoil.

INDEX

TO LEARN MORE

Finding more information is as easy as 1, 2, 3.

❶ Go to www.factsurfer.com

❷ Enter "foodscientist" into the search box.

❸ Click the "Surf" button to see a list of websites.

FACT SURFER